Nelson Mandela

A LIFE OF PERSISTENCE

by Jennifer Boothroyd

Lerner Publications Company • Minneapolis

Photo Acknowledgments

The photographs in this book are reproduced with the permission of: © UPPA/ZUMA Press, cover; © Walter Dhladhla/AFP/Getty Images, p. 4; © Guy Tillim/South Photo/The Bigger Picture, p. 6; © Hulton-Deutsch Collection/CORBIS, p. 7; © Bettmann/CORBIS, pp. 8, 10, 12, 19; © UWC RIM Mayibuye Archives, pp. 11, 13, 15; © Peter Magubane//Time Life Pictures/Getty Images, p. 14; © African Pictures/The Bigger Picture, pp. 16, 20; © Les Stone/ZUMA Press, p. 18; © ZUMA Archive/ZUMA Press, p. 21; © Allan Tannenbaum/ZUMA Press, 22; © Andrew Silk/ZUMA Press, p. 24; © Louise Gubb/CORBIS SABA, p. 25; © Jerzy Dabrowsky/ZUMA Press, p. 26.

Text copyright © 2007 by Lerner Publications Company

Lerner Publications Company
A division of Lerner Publishing Group
241 First Avenue North
Minneapolis, MN 55401 U.S.A.

Website address: www.lernerbooks.com

Words in **bold type** are explained in a glossary on page 31.

Library of Congress Cataloging-in-Publication Data

Boothroyd, Jennifer, 1972–
      Nelson Mandela : a life of persistence / by Jennifer Boothroyd.
          p.   cm. –   (Pull ahead books)
      Includes index.
      ISBN-13: 978–0–8225–6385–3 (lib. bdg. : alk. paper)
      ISBN-10: 0–8225–6385–1 (lib. bdg. : alk. paper)
      1. Mandela, Nelson, 1918– –Juvenile literature. 2. Presidents–South Africa–Biography–
Juvenile literature. 3. Persistence–Juvenile literature. I. Title. II. Series.
DT1974.B66 2007
968.06'5092–dc22   2006002452

Manufactured in the United States of America
1 2 3 4 5 6 – JR – 12 11 10 09 08 07

Table of Contents

Nelson Mandela helped change voting laws in South Africa.

Reaching a Goal

Think of a goal you worked hard to reach. It takes **persistence** to work hard and never give up. Nelson Mandela's persistence helped black people in South Africa get the same **rights** as whites.

Nelson was born in 1918 in a small South African village. His father was an important member of his **tribe**.

Nelson lived in a village like this one.

When Nelson grew up, he moved to
the city of Johannesburg.

Black South Africans lived in poor neighborhoods.

Unfair

Blacks and whites lived apart from one another in South Africa. Black South Africans did not have the same rights as white South Africans. Blacks couldn't vote. They could not go to the same schools or live in the same neighborhoods as whites. Nelson wanted to help blacks have better lives.

These people did not obey the *Europeans Only* sign on this train.

Nelson met other people who felt the same way he did. They did not **obey** laws that were unfair to blacks.

The police **arrested** Nelson many times. But he never stopped fighting for the rights of blacks.

Like Nelson, this woman was arrested for breaking a law.

One law required black people to carry special papers at all times.

In 1948, South African leaders
made laws that took away more of
blacks' rights.

Nelson spoke out against the new laws. The police arrested him again.

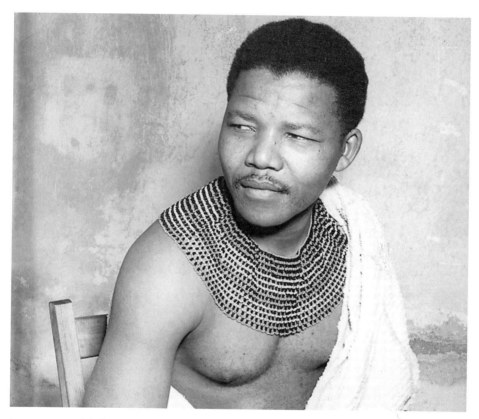

Nelson was proud to be a black South African.

Nelson gets out of jail.

The police set Nelson free. But the
government said he could not travel
or give speeches.

Nelson did not obey them. He went to other countries. He told people what was happening in South Africa.

Nelson traveled to London, England.

In jail, Nelson slept in a room like this one.

In Jail for Life

In 1962, the police arrested Nelson again. Then, just two years later, the government said he had to stay in jail for the rest of his life. Leaders did not want Nelson to say bad things about the government. They feared that more blacks would start breaking the law.

Americans heard about the problems in South Africa.

Word spread about the problems in South Africa.

People around the world wanted
Nelson set free.

Europeans protested how blacks were treated in South Africa.

Nelson worked for the rights of blacks while he was in jail.

Again, the government said Nelson could go free if he promised to obey the laws. He **refused**, so he had to stay in jail.

In 1989, South Africa **elected** a new president. He met with Nelson many times. They talked about the rights of black people.

South African president F. W. de Klerk

Nelson and his former wife, Winnie, celebrated his freedom.

Freedom

In 1990, President de Klerk let Nelson out of jail. Nelson had been in jail for 27 years. Together, Nelson and the president worked to change the laws that were unfair to blacks.

Blacks gained the right to vote.

Nelson worked with the government to make fair laws in South Africa.

The South African people elected
Nelson president in 1994. He worked
to bring peace to his country.

Nelson promised to work hard as president.

Persistence

Nelson's persistence helped him reach his goal. He faced many problems, but he never gave up fighting for the rights of blacks. He made his country a better place for people to live.

NELSON MANDELA TIMELINE

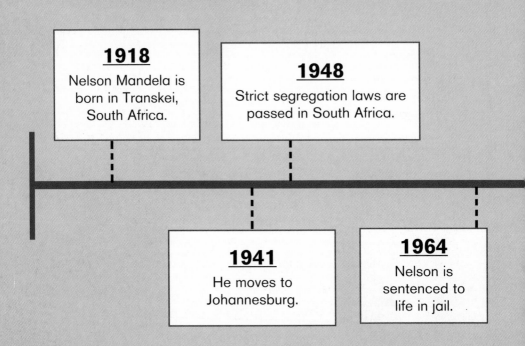

1918
Nelson Mandela is born in Transkei, South Africa.

1948
Strict segregation laws are passed in South Africa.

1941
He moves to Johannesburg.

1964
Nelson is sentenced to life in jail.

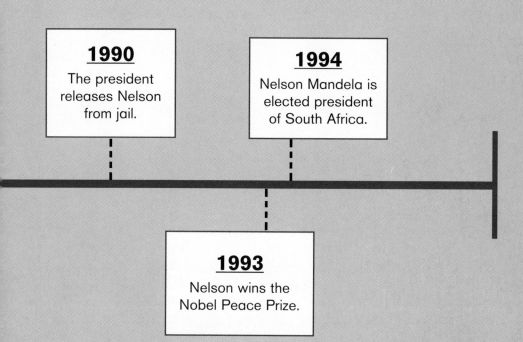

1990
The president releases Nelson from jail.

1994
Nelson Mandela is elected president of South Africa.

1993
Nelson wins the Nobel Peace Prize.

More about Nelson Mandela

● Nelson's parents named him Rolihlahla. When he was seven, his teacher gave him the name Nelson. The name has stayed with him throughout his life.

● F.W. de Klerk was the South African president who let Nelson out of jail. Both men won the Nobel Peace Prize for working together for peace.

● Before 1990, South African leaders believed in apartheid. *Apartheid* means "apartness" or "to separate people of different races." The leaders treated all people of color unfairly, not just blacks.

Websites

African National Congress
http://www.anc.org.za/people/mandela.html

Frontline: The Long Walk of Nelson Mandela
http://www.pbs.org/wgbh/pages/frontline/shows/man-dela/

The Nelson Mandela National Museum
http://www.nelsonmandelamuseum.org.za/

Glossary

arrested: taken to jail by the police

elected: chosen by voting

government: people who run a country

obey: to carry out or do what is asked

persistence: not giving up when working toward a goal

refused: would not

rights: the power to do something

tribe: a group of people who share a language and culture

Index